Spotlight on Reading

Summarizing

Grades 3–4

Carson-Dellosa Publishing LLC
Greensboro, North Carolina

Credits

Layout and Cover Design: Van Harris

Development House: The Research Masters

Cover Photo: Image Copyright StockLite, 2011 Used under license from Shutterstock.com

Visit *carsondellosa.com* for correlations to Common Core, state, national and Canadian provincial standards.

Carson-Dellosa Publishing LLC

PO Box 35665

Greensboro, NC 27425 USA

carsondellosa.com

ISBN 978-16-099-6496-2

13-333217784

About the Book

Summarizing is the skill of comprehending, focusing on important information, and rephrasing the information in a concise form. *Summarizing* for grades 3–4 contains guided activities that help students develop and achieve this skill. Students will identify the most important details to include in a summary along with writing their own summaries. As this skill is practiced in reading, students will naturally begin to use the skill in writing and speaking. Summarization is a concept used throughout the curriculum. Social studies, science, language, and reading all use the skill of summarization in written, read, and oral lessons.

This book is especially designed to help practice the concept of summarization by modeling examples of summaries and providing practice in pinpointing important events in stories, poems, and cartoons.

• •

Table of Contents

Name _____

Clever Boy, Wise Mom

Read the story. Complete sentences about the most important details from the story.

• •

Jimmy raced into the kitchen to his mother. He announced, "Sorry, Mom, but I won't be eating green food anymore. I just heard on the news that if you eat too much green food, you'll turn green too. So I won't be able to eat spinach, or peas, or even broccoli."

Jimmy grinned. He was sure that his mother would never guess he was just trying to get out of eating vegetables. He hated vegetables. He thought broccoli was the worst. But, he did not like peas, lettuce, cucumbers, or spinach very much either.

"I'm so sorry to hear that, Jimmy," his mother replied. "I guess that means you won't be having pistachio cupcakes or lime sherbet for dessert tonight." Jimmy's smile turned into a frown. Pistachio cupcakes and lime sherbet were not only green, they were his favorite foods. "After all Jimmy, I wouldn't want you to turn green," his mother said.

"You know what, Mom," Jimmy replied. "I think I misunderstood the news. They actually said that you have to eat green food to keep from turning green. So, I can have the cupcakes and the sherbet."

"You can also eat the broccoli I'm cooking," his mother replied.

"Right, that too," Jimmy said. His shoulders slumped. He walked back out of the kitchen. His mother watched him go with a laugh.

1. A little _____ did not like eating _____ .

2. So, he invented a _____ about how eating _____ food would turn him _____ .

3. He _____ because he thought he had tricked his mother.

4. However, his mother ruined his plan by serving _____ for dessert.

5. To eat the _____ , he would have to eat _____ too.

"Chewsing" a Dentist

Read the cartoon strip. Use words from the Word Bank to complete sentences about the most important details from the cartoon. Write the correct word on each line. Some words may be used more than once.

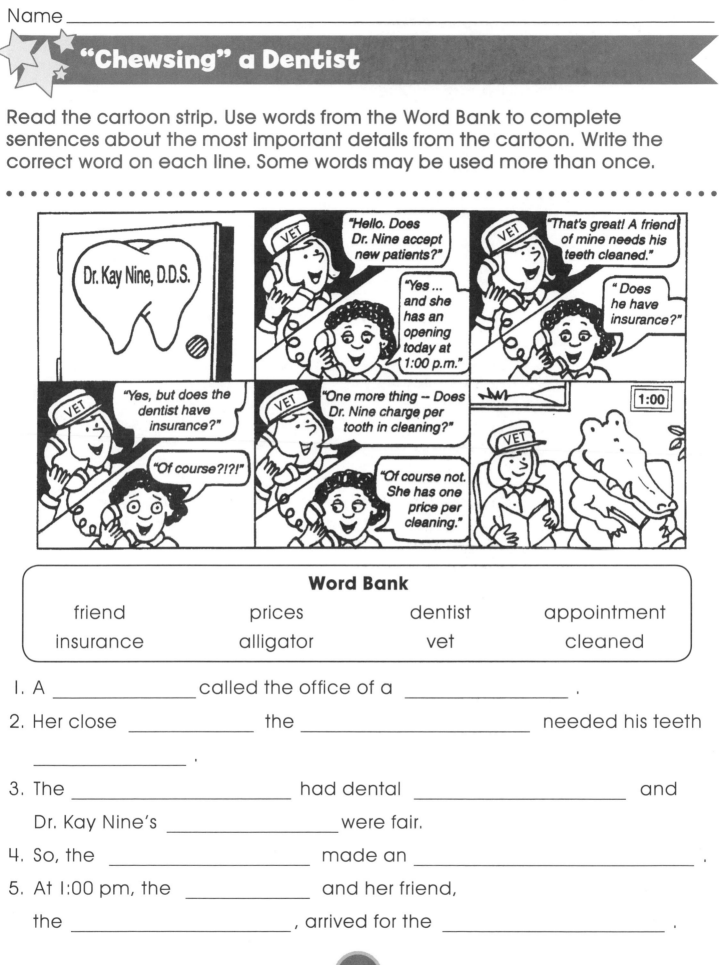

Word Bank

friend	prices	dentist	appointment
insurance	alligator	vet	cleaned

1. A _____ called the office of a _____ .

2. Her close _____ the _____ needed his teeth _____ .

3. The _____ had dental _____ and Dr. Kay Nine's _____ were fair.

4. So, the _____ made an _____ .

5. At 1:00 pm, the _____ and her friend, the _____ , arrived for the _____ .

Harry

Read the poem. Answer the questions.

• •

I have a special pet.
I love to watch him very much.
He's got silky, smooth hair
That I wouldn't want to touch.

His fur is blackish brown,
But combing is not at all necessary.
He is not at all beautiful but . . .
He is my best friend Harry.

Harry is not your average pet.
He eats flies by the pound!
He is usually very quiet,
Except for gurgling sounds.

Harry likes to explore a web,
But not the kind on a computer.
He is always on the move.
He likes to scale great heights.

I would love to be just like Harry.
Following him with all my might.
As Harry's eight legs travel oh so fast
We would soon be out of sight!

1. Check the sentence that best summarizes the poet's feelings about Harry.
   _____ a. The poet loves his pet spider Harry.
   _____ b. The poet is afraid of a spider hanging outside his window.
   _____ c. The poet is confused about a spider's weird habits and abilities.

2. Check the sentence that best summarizes what Harry can do.
   _____ a. Harry can use his eight legs to do lots of things.
   _____ b. Harry can use the computer and carry his owner on his back.
   _____ c. Harry can move fast, climb high, and eat weird things.

3. Check the sentence that best summarizes the entire poem.
   _____ a. Harry is an unusual pet with black fur and eight legs.
   _____ b. Harry is a hungry spider and has caught a fly in his web.
   _____ c. Harry is a scary spider and frightens everyone who sees him.

Super T Man

Read the story. Circle the correct answer for each question.

• •

Miguel's mother took him to the shopping mall. He wanted to go to the toy store to get a new video game. As Miguel reached the store, he saw his friend frowning.

"What's wrong?" Miguel asked.

Joe pointed to an action figure in the window. "They have Super T Man," he replied.

"That's great!" Miguel said. He also had been waiting for the Super T Man action figure.

"But, I don't have enough money to get it," Joe told his friend. "I spent my allowance on new sneakers."

"Well, don't sweat it," Miguel said. "I have enough money to buy one today. We can share mine until you get one of your own."

"You would do that for me?" Joe asked.

"Sure thing," Miguel replied.

"Someone needs to make a Super M Man action figure," Joe said.

"Who's Super M Man?'

"Miguel, my best friend!" Joe laughed. The two friends smiled as they walked into the toy store together.

1. What did Joe want?
   a. He wanted a pair of sneakers.
   b. He wanted an action figure.
   c. He wanted a video game.

2. What happened to Joe's money?
   a. He spent it at the toy store.
   b. He spent it at a school fair.
   c. He spent it on new sneakers.

3. How did Miguel help?
   a. He bought the action figure and shared it.
   b. He lent Joe money to buy an action figure.
   c. He promised to order an action figure online.

4. What is the best summary for this story?
   a. One friend helps another get a new toy.
   b. One friend takes another to the mall.
   c. One friend shows another a new video game.

Maya's Backpack Attack

Read the story. To complete the exercise, unscramble the letters of each word and write the correct word on the line.

• •

School starts tomorrow, so I should probably empty my lucky backpack. Mom said that we could buy another one. But I have had this backpack since second grade. I would never part with it! It has too many special memories! Hmmmm, let me see. Here is that spelling test from last October. I got an A on it.

Oooh! Here is my report on beetles from science class. I got a B on that one . . .

Wow, I forgot about the frog I got from my friend Perez. It hops when you touch its back. I love this ten-color pen. Too bad only three colors work. Here is that stuffed monkey that I borrowed from my friend Laurie. I will give it back to her tomorrow.

What is all this? There is a notebook, pencils, and a stick of gum near the bottom of the backpack. I think that is everything. My backpack looks pretty empty now. Wait a minute. I also see a sticky, gooey, chocolate cupcake from the last day of school. It is stuck to the bottom. What a mess! "Hey, Mom, maybe I should get a new backpack after all!" Maya called out.

School was starting. So, _____ needed to clean her lucky
ayMa

_____. Inside she found many things. She found a _____ test,
kkaaccbp   lsinpegl

a hopping _____ , a _____ about beetles, a stuffed
grfo   ertpor

_____, and a ten-color _____. She also found _____,
ykoenm   epn   slpneic

a _____, and a stick of _____. When she felt a _____
koonbeto   mgu   ckitsy

mess, she decided she needed a _____ backpack after all.
wen

Vroo-o-o-m!

Read the cartoon strip. Use words from the Word Bank to complete a summary of the cartoon. Write the correct word on each line. Some words may be used more than once.

Word Bank

rubber	car	bridge	wings
wheel	water	laughs	tires

Axle Rod Jones is building a special _____. First, he fastens

on the steering _____. Then he bolts on four special _____.

They can burn _____. Finally, he ties on some _____.

Axle tells his friend that the car can travel over _____.

Then he drives across a _____. Axle's friend _____

when he realizes he has been tricked.

9

Ride, Cowboy, Ride!

Read the story. Place a check on the line beside the answer for each question.

• •

Ever since my friend Bobby visited a horse ranch, he has become a different person. He does not want us to call him Bobby anymore. Instead, he wants us to use the nickname Buck. I do not know what to think. This is all very confusing.

Now, the only kind of shoes Buck wears are cowboy boots! His favorite powder blue boots match the blue sky on the open range. Buck told me that he even sleeps in boots. That way, he can go to bed with his shoes on. He says that is how horses do it. They never take off their horseshoes. Of course, each pair of boots has a matching shirt and hat.

Yesterday, Buck attached a toy horse head and tail to his bike. He claimed that it would give him extra "horsepower." I am convinced Buck is not just "horsing around." Buck may actually become a cowboy when he grows up!

1. Which sentence best summarizes why Buck wants to be a cowboy?
    _____ a. Buck's best friend is a cowboy.
    _____ b. Buck watches lots of cowboy movies.
    _____ c. Buck recently visited a horse ranch.

2. Which sentence best summarizes how Buck's friend reacts?
    _____ a. His friend is confused about Buck.
    _____ b. His friend wants to be like Buck.
    _____ c. His friend is angry at Buck.

3. Which sentence best summarizes the entire story?
    _____ a. Buck wants to be a cowboy, and his friend thinks it is a good idea.
    _____ b. Buck dresses and acts like a cowboy and his friend is confused.
    _____ c. Buck told his friend about the horse ranch and now they both want to be cowboys.

Summarizing • CD-104560

Presto Chango!

Read the cartoon strip and the summary about it. Cross out any sentences that contain unnecessary details for retelling the story. Then answer the question below.

• •

A young magician performed magic tricks. She was called the Great Hoodwinker. First, she made a big, juicy apple disappear. It looked big and juicy. She ate it. Next, she announced that some tacks would float up into the air. She used a magnet to lift them up. It was a large, horseshoe magnet. Last, she pulled a hair from her magic hat. The audience probably thought she meant "hare" as in "rabbit."

1. Check the sentence that best summarizes the entire cartoon strip.

    _____ a. The Great Hoodwinker is an excellent magician.

    _____ b. This magician fooled the audience by tricking them with the words she used.

    _____ c. It is difficult to understand how the Great Hoodwinker performs her tricks.

Name _____

What Would It Be Like?

Read the poem. Circle the verse that contains the introduction. Draw a box around the verse that contains the conclusion. Complete the activity on page 13.

• •

What Would It Be Like?

When I am on the edge of sleep,
I close my eyes in bed.
Suddenly, I begin to change.
I become an animal instead.

It happens when I shut my eyes tight
While I lie quietly on my back.
I am no longer a short boy
Now, I am a big and hairy yak.

A yak is kind of like a furry cow
That is strong and can climb and jump,
My friends are shocked to see,
My four legs, two horns, and furry
   hump!

Next, I change into something else,
That makes me laugh and laugh.
My neck starts to stretch and stretch.
Until I turn into a giraffe.

I am the tallest of all of my friends.
It is nice not to be so small.
I am big enough to see over a fence,
Or look onto a roof or over a wall!

The next change is even better.
My head starts to turn bright yellow.
I grow a long beak and wings, too.
I become a bird called a hoopoe
   (HOO-poo)!

I wear a crown of feathers on my
   head.
My body has bold stripes of black
   and white
But best of all I spread my wings,
And I take to the skies in flight.

Then all of a sudden, it is time to
   wake up,
I am back to being just a boy.
I like to think about being an animal.
It gives me so much joy.

I know so many math facts.
Science is so easy for me!
But dreaming my dreams is so much
   fun.
I can be anything that I see!

I might be small and kind of short.
I have no hump, long neck, or wings.
But if I dream that I can have them,
I can do quite amazing things!

What Would It Be Like? (cont.)

Number the sentences in the correct order to create a summary of the poem.

• •

_____ a. A boy fell asleep in his bed.

_____ b. The boy became a bird called a hoopoe.

_____ c. The boy woke up from his dream.

_____ d. Next, the boy turned into a giraffe with a long neck.

_____ e. The boy dreamed he was a yak.

The Very Best!

Try this: On another sheet of paper, write a summary of the poem in your own words.

13

★ Seeds, Seeds, Seeds

Read the passage. Answer questions about the most important details.

• •

Many plants begin their lives as seeds. Flowers, garden vegetables, and trees all grow from seeds. As they develop, they sprout new seeds that can be planted in soil to grow more plants. Try soaking a lima bean in water and then cutting it in half. You will see a baby plant inside of a seed.

Seeds come in many sizes. A coconut is one example of a very big seed. Coconuts are a tasty fruit that grow on tropical islands in palm trees. As they turn ripe, they fall off the tree. Coconuts are not just big, they can also float. They often float on the sea to other islands where they can grow into new palm trees.

Palm trees are big, but big plants do not always come from big seeds. A redwood, one of the biggest trees in the world, grows from a very tiny seed. The seeds grow inside pine cones on the branches of redwood trees.

After seeds leave a plant, they need a good place to grow. They usually need rich soil and lots of water and sunlight to grow. Some seeds need to be planted quickly. When seeds fall off a willow tree, they die after a few days if they are not planted in the ground. Other seeds last much longer. The seeds of a lotus flower will still grow after a thousand years!

I.   What is this article about? _____

2.   What happens when you plant a coconut? _____

3.   Which tree has a bigger seed, a palm tree or a redwood tree? _____

_____

4.   How are willow seeds different from lotus flower seeds? _____

_____

5.   Write a short summary of this article. _____

_____

_____

Breakfast of Winners

Read the letter. Circle the best summary of the letter.

. . . .

"Why Crunchy Munchy Bunches of Bananas and Bran Flakes is My Favorite Cereal" Contest.

Dear Cereal Maker,

I try to eat your delicious cereal every day. It is my second choice for breakfast. My first choice is cold pizza. But, Mom says I can only eat that on my birthday.

Why do I like your cereal so much? First of all, I love that it tastes like bananas. Mom says that I act like a monkey when I climb on the furniture. And we all know that monkeys love bananas.

Second, my big brother always tells me not to act so flaky! And your cereal has lots of big corn flakes. Anyway, I guess I cannot help liking your cereal! I hope I win this contest.

Your friend,
Horace

Summary A

A child has written a letter to his best friend. He tells his friend that she should try eating Crunchy Munchy cereal for breakfast. He says that it has the best mix of banana flavor and corn flakes.

Summary B

A child has written a letter to enter a contest. He explains why Crunchy Munchy is his favorite cereal. He says he likes it because he acts like a monkey and monkeys like bananas.

Summary C

A child has written a letter to a cereal company. He wants them to make more Crunchy Munchy cereal. He eats their cereal every day of the year except for his birthday.

Three Stories

Read these three stories. Choose the sentence that provides the best summary for each story. Write the letter of each correct answer on the blank line.

• •

_____ 1. Laura has been watching her mother knit a sweater for weeks. When she asked for the sweater, she did not know how long it would take. Laura only knew she wanted something blue and fluffy to wear skiing. As she watches, she feels guilty for asking. Laura thinks her mother is so sweet to take that much time to make something for her! So, she offers to do more chores to help out.

a. Laura's mother teaches her how to knit a sweater.

b. Laura's mother goes out of her way to knit a sweater.

c. Laura does not want to do extra chores around the house.

_____ 2. Cookouts are fun in the summer. People bring their favorite foods. Some like to grill hot dogs and toast buns. Others like to grill eggplants and other vegetables. Either way, the food tastes great! Cookouts are not only about the food. People often play softball and other games.

a. There are lots of ways to make hot dogs.

b. Some people do not like grilled vegetables.

c. Summer cookouts are a lot of fun.

_____ 3. Peter is a penguin with a big problem. He hates to walk on the ice because he always slips and falls. But, ice completely covers the ground where he lives. It is impossible to avoid it. His friend Polly offers to help him out. She buys him a pair of ice skates. It is much easier for Peter to skate on the ice than to walk on it. Now, he never has to worry about slipping or falling down.

a. Polly buys Peter skates to keep him from slipping on ice.

b. Peter is a penguin, but his friend Polly is a different kind of bird.

c. Polly the penguin gave her friend Peter ice skating lessons.

Name _____

Space Probes

Read the passage. Choose from a list of ideas to include in a summary about the article. Place a check on the line next to all your choices.

• •

   We learn about planets by watching them. But, planets are very far away. Scientists use telescopes to see them. A telescope is a special instrument. It makes things that are far away look closer.

   Some planets are too far away to see clearly. They are too hard to watch, even with a telescope. How do we learn about them? Scientists send machines called probes into space. Cameras are sent in the probe. They take pictures of everything they see.

   Probes also carry tools. These tools study the weather on other planets. They study the rocks and soil too. All of the pictures and information are sent back to Earth. Scientists study them to learn more about planets and space.

   The first probe to study a planet was called Mariner 2. It was sent into space in 1962. It gave us information about the planet Venus. Since then, scientists have sent dozens of probes into space. Each one tells us more and more about other planets.

_____ a. Planets are very far away from Earth.

_____ b. Scientists use telescopes to see planets.

_____ c. Scientists also send probes to planets.

_____ d. Cameras are also useful to scientists.

_____ e. Weather on other planets is interesting.

_____ f. Probes send pictures of planets back to Earth.

_____ g. The very first probe was sent to Venus.

_____ h. The first probe had a funny name.

Ellie and Polly

Read the story. Complete activities on page 19.

• •

Ellie and her dog Polly walked in the hot sun. Ellie was sweating, but she kept walking happily. Polly did not know where they were going. But, she would go where Ellie went. When they arrived at the ice cream shop, there was a long line. As they got in line, Ellie looked ahead. There were 10 people in front of them. It was so hot! It was sure hard to wait!

Polly looked around the shop. She noticed a white dog that seemed interesting. She wanted to go over to the other dog. But, Ellie grabbed her collar and told Polly, "No, stay here with me."

Ellie took another look at the line. Now, there were only five people in front of them. She did not need to think about what to order because she knew just what she wanted. Ellie wiped the sweat off her forehead. Polly was hot too.

After a few more minutes, they were next in line. Ellie was excited. Polly brushed up against Ellie's leg and tried to push her ahead. Ellie scratched Polly's neck. "You're right, girl. We're up next."

Finally, it was their turn. Ellie walked up to the counter and said, "I'll have a cone of chocolate chip, please. And may I have a bowl of water for my friend?"

"Sure thing," the clerk said.

After getting their order, Ellie and Polly went to a table. Ellie ate her ice cream while Polly drank her water. It was the perfect thing to have on a hot, summer day.

Ellie and Polly (cont.)

Circle the best summary of the story. Then draw a picture of Ellie and Polly in the box.

. . . .

Summary A

A girl and her dog go on a long walk on a summer day. They pass by many places in their neighborhood, including an ice cream shop.

Summary B

A dog chases another dog through an ice cream shop and makes her owner very angry. Ice cream spills all over the floor.

Summary C

A girl takes her dog to the park. They stop by an ice cream truck to buy a cone and a bottle of water.

Summary D

A girl and her dog visit an ice cream shop. They order a cone and a bowl of water to cool off on a summer day.

The Wright Brothers

Read the passage. Complete the activity on page 21.

• •

Orville and Wilbur Wright were famous American brothers. They owned a bicycle shop in Ohio. They loved bicycles. But, they also loved the idea of flying. In 1896, they began to experiment, or try new ideas, with flight.

First, they started by testing kites. Then, they worked on gliders, which are planes without motors. These tests showed them how an airplane should move. They learned how it should rise, turn, and come back to the ground. The brothers flew their gliders at Kitty Hawk. That is a beach in North Carolina. It was very windy there. That helped their gliders take off.

In 1903, they created a machine that they called The Flyer. It had a motor and was their first airplane. The Flyer was large and heavy. The brothers could not rely on wind to help it fly, so they built a track for it. They wheeled The Flyer along the track to help it take off.

In December 1903, the Wright Brothers were ready to test The Flyer. The plane lifted about ten feet off the ground. It flew over the sand for a short time. Then, it landed back on the ground. The Flyer only traveled about 120 feet (36.5 meters). But, it had flown! The brothers continued to work on their plane. After awhile, it could stay in the air for over one hour.

Other inventors followed the work of the Wright brothers. They looked for ways to improve airplanes. They helped planes fly faster and longer. They also worked to make planes bigger to fit more people. Today, hundreds of planes take to the sky each day. People fly to go across the country or across the seas. We have the Wright brothers to thank for the first flight.

The Wright Brothers (cont.)

Answer questions about the passage on page 20.

· ·

1. What is the most important idea in this article?
   a. Experimenting and testing new ideas is important.
   b. The Wright brothers called their plane The Flyer.
   c. The Wright brothers were the first people to fly.

2. Where did the brothers test their gliders and plane?

   _____

3. How far was their first flight with a motor?

   _____

4. Write a short summary of the article.

   _____

   _____

   _____

   _____

21

"Fangs" a Lot!

Read two letters. Complete the activities on page 23.

• •

Dear Tooth Fairy,

   I think that over the years you have collected a lot of teeth. My brother, sister, and I have already added at least twenty teeth to your collection. What do you do with all those teeth? Do you make sets of false teeth with them? Do they use them for dummies at the department store?
   Also, I would like to know if you only collect people's teeth. What happens to shark and alligator teeth? They would make a really "sharp" collection!
   Please, write back!

Love,
Jamal

Dear Jamal,

   Thanks for your letter. You ask very interesting questions. I do not use my collection to make false teeth. I also do not give them to department stores. Instead, I turn them into wishes that make children happy. Also, sharks and alligators do not put their teeth under pillows like little boys and girls. Instead, their teeth fall into the water. They are collected by the Tooth Fairy Fish.
   Love,
   The Tooth Fairy

"Fangs" a Lot! (cont.)

Circle the best summary for each letter.

Jamal's Letter
Summary 1
   Jamal writes a letter to the tooth fairy to find out what happens to the teeth in her collection.

Summary 2
   Jamal writes a letter to the tooth fairy to find out when he will get money for his loose tooth.

Summary 3
   Jamal writes a letter to the tooth fairy to find out when she will visit again.

The Tooth Fairy's Letter
Summary 1
   The tooth fairy replies that she also has shark teeth in her collection.

Summary 2
   The tooth fairy replies that she does not owe Jamal any money for his teeth.

Summary 3
   The tooth fairy replies that she turns her collection of teeth into wishes.

Try this: Write a more complete summary of each letter. Include more details.

Growing Up

Read the story. Complete the activity on page 25.

• •

By the time he was nine years old, Joey thought he had outgrown most of his toys. He decided to sell them at his family's garage sale. Joey started to clean his room, going through his bedroom closet.

"I remember this old truck," he said to himself. "Grandpa and Grandma gave it to me when I turned five. I think Grandpa had as much fun as I did. We used it to dump sand in the sandbox. The truck got a little rusty, but it always worked fine."

Joey put the truck into a bag and pushed aside some clothes. He uncovered a shiny, blue and white yo-yo. "I remember thinking this yo-yo was broken when I first tried it," Joey recalled. "Then I practiced and realized nothing was wrong with it." He had even taught his younger brother Josh a few tricks with it. Little by little, the bag on the floor began to fill up.

Finally, at the bottom of the closet, was his well-worn teddy bear, Herbie. "I know I'm definitely too old for this!" Joey said to himself. "Teddy bears are for little kids." Joey picked up Herbie and dropped him into the bag of unwanted toys.

Joey leaned up against the bed to look over what he had collected. He stared inside the bag, and his eyes focused on Herbie. "Herbie and I had a lot of fun together," Joey recalled. "I remember when Dad, Mom, and Josh brought him to the hospital when I had my tonsils removed. My throat was sore, and I was so scared. And Herbie sure knew how to make me feel better during storms. When lightning and thunder woke me up I would pull the covers over my head. Then I would hug Herbie so I wouldn't feel scared."

Joey gazed at Herbie one more time and then began thinking about other items in the bag. "Actually, maybe I'm not too old for these things. After all, they're still in pretty good shape!"

He carried the bag to his closet, dumped its contents in the back, and then grabbed the yo-yo. "Hey, Josh!" he called to his older brother. "Let's play with my yo-yo. Maybe I can teach you a few new tricks."

⭐ Growing Up (cont.)

Choose words from the Word Bank to complete a summary of the story on page 24. You may need to use some words more than once.

- -

Word Bank

sell	broken	grandparents	truck	friend
yo-yo	old	teddy bear	look	keep

Joey felt that he was too _____ for most of his toys. So, he decided

to _____ them. He began to _____ through his closet.

First, Joey found an old _____ that his _____

had given him. Next, he discovered a _____. He had thought it was

_____ until he learned how to use it. Finally, Joey pulled out an

old _____. It had been his best _____ when he was a

little boy. After thinking about it, Joey decided to _____ his old

toys for a while. He realized that maybe he was not too _____

for them after all.

⭐ Picture Time

Read the story. Complete the activity on page 27.

• •

The time had come for the big class photo. Mr. Hallam, the photographer, had already done individual pictures of the fourth graders. He thought the last class would be a snap, as he liked to say. But, things did not go exactly as planned.

Mrs. Martinez called out to her class. "Now, you each have a brush or a comb. Please use them to get ready for the picture." The students fidgeted as they all got ready.

Suddenly, the fire alarm sounded. "OK, everyone," Mrs. Martinez said. "That means we're having a fire drill. You know what to do." With Mrs. Martinez in the lead, the students filed out the of the classroom. Mr. Hallam was right behind.

As they stepped outside in the sunny day, Mr. Hallam got an idea. "Hey, this would be the perfect place to take a picture," he told Mrs. Martinez. "What do you think?"

"Sounds like a great idea to me," she replied.

So, all the fourth graders got together to take the picture. But, just as Mr. Hallam held up his camera, a breeze began to blow. It blew everyone's hair out of place. The picture was ruined!

"Well, that didn't work," Mr. Hallam said. "Can you all fix your hair again?" The students did. They took out their brushes and combs. They straightened their hair and fixed their ribbons. Then they got ready to take another picture.

But as Mr. Hallam held up his camera, a breeze began to blow again. This time, it was even stronger. It blew everyone's hair out of place again. It also swirled fallen leaves into the air. They blew all around in front of the students. The picture was ruined again!

"Can we try one more time?" Mr. Hallam asked. "The third time will be the charm."

The students took out their combs and brushes one last time. They straightened their hair and fixed their ribbons. They smoothed down their curls and tightened their braids. Then they got ready to take another picture.

Picture Time (cont.)

After finishing the story, number the sentences in order from 1 to 10 to complete a summary of the story.

• •

But as Mr. Hallam held up his camera, a breeze began to blow again. It was even stronger than the first two times. It blew everyone's hair. It swirled fallen leaves into the air. It even scattered a flock of birds from a nearby tree. The breeze made a great big mess!

Everything looked so crazy, the students started to laugh. They all laughed and laughed. They looked like they were having such a fun time. Mr. Hallam thought, "What a great picture that would make." So, he held up his camera and finally snapped the picture.

Everyone loved the way the picture turned out. It was not a perfect photo. But, it was the most fun out of all of the fourth grade pictures.

_____ a. Mr. Hallam finally snaps the picture.

_____ b. Everyone loves the photo of Mrs. Martinez's class.

_____ c. A strong breeze begins to blow for the second time.

_____ d. Everyone's hair gets messy for the first time.

_____ e. Leaves swirl into the air for the second time.

_____ f. The school fire alarm goes off.

_____ g. A flock of birds scatters from a tree.

_____ h. Students comb their hair in the classroom.

_____ i. Mr. Hallam decides to take the picture outside.

_____ j. The class leaves the school and goes outside.

Helen Keller

Read the passage. Complete the activity on page 29.

• •

Helen Keller was a well-known woman. She was born in 1880. When she was just 19 months old, she became very sick. Her illness left her blind and deaf. That meant that she was unable to see or hear. Her world became a dark, quiet place. She began to feel angry and afraid. As a result, she started to have temper tantrums and act wildly.

Helen's parents wanted to help her. They hired a teacher named Annie Sullivan. Annie understood what it meant to be blind. She found a way to teach Helen. Annie taught Helen to "hear" and "speak" with her hands. Helen even learned how to use her voice and speak.

Helen was very smart and dedicated. She became a very good student. She went to college and graduated with honors. When she became an adult, Helen wrote books and gave many speeches.

Helen Keller also worked to help others. She taught other people how to cope with being blind or deaf. She also worked against unfairness and violence. Helen won awards for all of the good things she did. She became very famous and lived to be 88 years old.

Helen Keller (cont.)

Answer questions about the passage on page 28.

• •

1. What is the most important idea in this article?

    a. Helen Keller learned how to hear and speak with her "hands."

    b. Helen Keller wrote books and gave speeches.

    c. Helen Keller became sick when she was 19 months old.

2. How did an illness affect Helen Keller?

    _____

3. Who helped Helen Keller learn how to speak?

    _____

4. Write a short summary of the article.

    _____

    _____

    _____

    _____

It's What?

Read the story. Complete the activity on page 31.

• •

Last Friday began as any other normal day during summer vacation. My little sister Makayla and I scrambled out of bed. We got dressed and quickly ate our breakfast. Then we darted out the door.

The first thing we did was bounce on our new trampoline. Makayla and I have both improved. We are learning to perfect our knee drops.

Soon we lost interest and decided to in-line skate. We strapped on our helmets. Mine is an awesome purple and Makayla's is electric green. Then we fastened our elbow and knee pads and tightened the buckles on our blades. I called out, "Let's roll!" Several neighbors joined us, including our friend Sally. We pretended we were in a roller derby. Eventually, boredom struck. Once again, we decided to do something different.

Hopscotch sounded fun, so we gathered colored chalk and started to play. After my little sister won three games straight, Sally and I talked about what to do next.

The three of us tried jumping rope. But, Makayla kept missing. She complained that I was not twirling the rope correctly. So, we hung the jump rope on a hook in the garage. As Sally headed for home, my sister and I plopped down on the front porch steps.

"Summer is so-o-o-o-o boring," I said quite wearily. "There is never anything fun to do," Makayla added..

Soon, we started to get hungry. "We'd better go inside and see what Mom has made for our lunch," I declared. We ran to the kitchen.

"Mom, what's for lunch?" asked Makayla. Mom answered, "It's macaroni and cheese. I decided to make your favorite lunch because you know what happens next week."

"Huh?" I groggily replied, scratching my head. "What's happening next week?" "School begins on Monday," reminded Mom. Makayla and I froze in our tracks. "But, Mom," I whined. "There's so much more we have left to do this summer!"

Makayla and I looked at each other. Reality set in. We loved summer. We could not believe it was over already.

It's What?

Read this summary of the story on page 30. Draw a line through any sentences that may be interesting but are not needed to retell the story.

• •

Last Friday, my sister Makayla and I woke and got ready to play. We ate our favorite energy-boosting breakfast.

The first thing we did was jump on the trampoline. We jumped very high and improved our drops.

When that became boring, we gathered some neighbors and began to in-line skate. It was fun to pretend we were competing in a roller derby. I just love to "lead the pack" around the block.

Next, we chose to hopscotch. This is Makayla's favorite activity because she always seems to win. I lost interest quickly because I always seem to lose. Maybe a lucky rock would help me.

Once again, we became bored, so we sat on the front porch. Soon, it was time for lunch. Our friend Sally went home and we walked into our kitchen. Mom had made our favorite meal. I could eat macaroni and cheese almost any time. Makayla loves it too.

Then, Mom announced that school begins next week. Thoughts of all we had left to do during our vacation floated through our minds.

Name _____

Read the passage. Complete the activity on page 33.

• •

There are about 600 million cars around the world. Cars first became popular in the early 1900s. Many early cars were built in a factory owned by a man named Henry Ford. He made cars that were low enough in price that many people could afford them.

Ford's cars looked different from the cars you see on the road now. Many were convertibles. The top folded up or down. There were only two seats in the car. There was one long seat in the front and one long seat in the back. Also, many of the cars did not have bumpers or mirrors. That's because those things cost extra money. Adding them made a car more expensive.

There were other differences too. Ford's cars did use gas. But the gas tank was under the driver's seat. That means people had to lift the seat to put gas in the car. Sometimes, the cars would not start in cold weather. To get them to start, people poured hot water under the hood.

Today, cars are very different. They look a lot more like the drawing below. Cars from long ago also could not go as fast as the cars we drive today. But, they looked like a lot of fun to ride!

Name _____

Now or Then (cont.)

Number the sentences in order from 1 to 5 to complete a summary of the passage. Draw a picture of one of Henry Ford's cars in the box.

• •

_____ a. Cars today are much faster than cars from the past.

_____ b. Henry Ford made cars that many people could afford.

_____ c. Cars first became popular in the early 1900s.

_____ d. The gas tank of Ford's cars was under the driver's seat.

_____ e. Ford's cars looked different from the cars of today.

The Big Game

Read the story. Complete the activity on page 35.

• •

Cranebrook Heights and Mareville were different neighborhoods. Cranebrook was near the river. Mareville was close to the woods. But the communities had two important things in common.

The first was a big park. It had been there forever. It sat right in the middle of the two neighborhoods. The park had a huge soccer field, which was the second thing the neighborhoods had in common. Cranebrook kids and Mareville kids loved soccer.

One hot summer, things got tense. Here and there a word would get said. There was talk about how one neighborhood was better than another. The leader of the Cranebrook kids was a boy named Peter. Katya was the one the Mareville kids all listened to. One day, Peter and Katya met in the park.

"We have to do something," Peter said. He wiped the back of his neck. "If this summer gets any hotter, things will explode."

Katya had a soccer ball. She kicked it to Peter. "I know. But what can we do about it?"

They played for a half hour. At the end, they were hot and tired—but happy.

"Hey," Katya said. "I think I've got an idea." Katya told Peter her idea. They could have a big soccer game. That would help bring everyone together. They could have grown-up referees from both neighborhoods. That way, the game would be fair.

"I like it," Peter said. "But will it really work?"

For the next two weeks, all anyone talked about was the big game. Both teams practiced whenever they could. The game would decide who would win the honor of best team.

Then a remarkable thing happened. Both sides practiced in the park each day. But when Cranebrook Heights players saw Mareville players, they did not argue or fight. Instead, they high-fived each other. "Working hard?" they would say to one another. They all had something to do, and something to look forward to.

When game day came, the August day was hotter than ever. Families came to watch from all over the city. The game was fierce. Cranebrook scored an early point. Then, Mareville tied the score. Mareville got ahead. But, in the last minute, Cranebrook scored another goal. The teams were tied!

The Big Game (cont.)

Finish reading the story and then complete the summary below the story by circling each correct word or phrase.

• •

There were only minutes left in the game. Would one of the teams score a winning goal? As a buzzer sounded, the game was over. The score was tied 3 to 3. No one had won! But it did not matter. They all enjoyed the game.

Peter went over to Katya. "I never thought I'd see it," Peter said. "It's like we're all from the same neighborhood." Katya smiled. "I think today we are," she said.

There were two neighborhoods. One, called _____Cranebrook / Mareville_____, had big

houses and a private school. The other called _____Cranebrook / Mareville_____ had a public

school. But kids in both places loved the same thing— _____playing soccer / eating candy_____ .

They also shared a big _____beach / park_____. When things got tense between the

kids, leaders from both neighborhoods, Peter and _____Katya / Carla_____, met to decide

what to do. They agreed to hold a big soccer game. The two teams met in

the park on a _____windy / hot_____ August day. _____Teachers / Families_____ came from all over the city

to watch. The game was a _____loss / tie_____. In the end, Peter and Katya both felt

like all the kids were from _____the same / a different_____ neighborhood.

Read the first part of a story. Complete the activities on page 37.

Mrs. Bradford smiled broadly as she let me in the house. "Cassie, you don't realize how grateful Mr. Bradford and I are to see you! We know you have finals at the community college. We were afraid we wouldn't be able to get a babysitter on such short notice. We will be home about midnight. Here's a list of instructions and an emergency number to call if necessary."

"Bye, Bettie!" Mr. and Mrs. Bradford both said. "Be sure to listen to Cassie!" They kissed their daughter on the cheek and left.

After they left, I read Mrs. Bradford's note. It said:

Cassie,
1. Warm spaghetti in the microwave and feed Bettie.
2. Give Bettie a bath and put on her pajamas.
3. Play a game with Bettie.
4. Put Bettie to bed.
5. Relax and watch television until we return.

"Simple enough," I thought as I put the note down and headed for the kitchen to feed Bettie.

I found the spaghetti in the refrigerator. As I placed the container in the microwave, little Bettie stood in front of the open refrigerator and put her hands in a bowl of chocolate pudding. "No, Bettie!" I said firmly as I pulled her away.

"Cassie want some?" Bettie asked as she laid her hands on my mouth and all across my face. I knew she was trying to be nice, but she still made a mess.

I quickly wiped her hands and my face and lowered her into her chair. After heating the spaghetti, I began to feed her dinner.

"Ooh, yummy, yummy!" Bettie clearly loved to eat spaghetti. She loved it so much that she grabbed some off her plate and threw it into the air! It landed everywhere, including my hair. "Uh-oh," Bettie said with a big smile.

The Babysitting Blues—Part One (cont.)

"Bettie! Come back!" I yelled as I chased her into the living room, leaving a trail of spaghetti as I went. I finally caught her at the piano rubbing her hands across the keys. She said she wanted to play a song for me because she liked me so much. I thought that was nice. But she left spaghetti all over the piano. That meant I had even more mess to clean up!

I carried Bettie back to the kitchen and fed her the little bit of spaghetti left in the bowl. Then, I checked the first item off Mrs. Bradford's list. Next on the list was Bettie's bath. She certainly needed one. This time I was not going to let her out of my sight.

1. Briefly describe Cassie.

    _____

    _____

    _____

    _____

2. Briefly describe Bettie.

    _____

    _____

    _____

    _____

3. Write a brief summary of the three ways that Bettie created mischief for Cassie.

    a. _____

    b. _____

    c. _____

Now, read the next part of the story!

The Babysitting Blues—Part Two

Read the rest of the story. Complete the activities on page 39.

I carried Bettie while I got a towel and her pajamas. I even held her while I ran the bath water. I poured a small amount of bubble bath into the tub. As I lowered Bettie into the water, she grabbed the bubble bath. Then, she dumped the whole thing into the tub! "Oh, well," I thought. "At least she'll get really clean."

Soon, bubbles were everywhere! Bettie splashed and splashed until everything was wet. Next, I rinsed off Bettie, took her out of the tub and dried her. Finally, I put on her pajamas. Then, I checked off the second item on my list.

"Hmmm," I wondered as I checked the list again. "What kind of game should we play?" "Cassie build a house!" Bettie shouted. "Okay, Bettie," I agreed, "but you have to sit perfectly still!" I was surprised that she listened as I used blocks to build four walls around her. "This was pretty easy," I thought.

But I had spoken too soon. Bettie suddenly stood up. "Let me help!" Bettie yelled. "I take house apart." Then, she kicked the blocks and sent them flying around the room.

I groaned as I checked item number three from my list. Then, I told her, "It's time for bed." I carried Bettie to her bedroom. Amazingly, she fell asleep right away. She must have been really tired after making all that mess.

After Bettie was asleep, I cleaned and cleaned until all the mess was gone. It took hours. When I finally finished, I plopped down on the sofa. Just then, I heard the front door open.

"Cassie, we're back," said Mr. Bradford.

"The house looks great!" said Mrs. Bradford. "By the way, we would like to know if you can come back again tomorrow."

"Uh, I don't think so, Mrs. Bradford. I'm pretty busy." I felt badly that I could not help them out. But I just could not babysit for Bettie again. I have never seen a child who tries to be good act so bad!

The Babysitting Blues—Part Two (cont.)

1. Briefly summarize two times that Bettie created mischief for Cassie.

    a. _____

    _____

    b. _____

    _____

2. Here is Mrs. Bradford's list of jobs for Cassie. Number the jobs in the order of their occurrence in the story.

    _____ Put Bettie to bed.

    _____ Give Bettie a bath.

    _____ Warm spaghetti and feed Bettie.

    _____ Relax. Watch television until we return.

    _____ Play a game or play with toys.

    Try This: Write a list of helpful tips for babysitters.

Frank and Beanie

My family was the first to arrive at Uncle Frank and Aunt Beanie's annual family barbeque, so we helped get everything ready. Uncle Frank asked me to set up the lawn chairs. As I was putting them around the lawn and pool, Uncle Frank said, "Set the bright orange chair on the line directly in front of the pool. Sit down and push the green button on the armrest as soon as you are comfortable."

I did as I was told. As I sat in the chair, I pushed the button. It began to softly vibrate. Then I started bouncing up and down in my seat. All of a sudden, the chair's seat popped up and gently flung me into the pool! When I came out of the water, I was laughing uncontrollably. It was another of Uncle Frank's fantastic inventions.

After I dried off, Aunt Beanie called for me to help her in the kitchen. I wrapped a towel around my waist and ran inside. "Do you want to see Uncle Frank's latest creation?" she asked me. I nodded.

She led me to what appeared to be a tiny roller coaster sitting on the kitchen table.

"This isn't a toy if that's what you're thinking," she said. "It's *Uncle Frank's Savor the Flavor – Roller Coaster Condiments Machine.* Let's try it."

Aunt Beanie placed a hot dog in a bun and put it inside a car on the coaster. "Let's see," she said as she began pushing some buttons. "This hot dog needs the works!" Slowly, the car went down the tracks. After it climbed the first hill, bright red ketchup squirted. Spicy mustard sprayed out of a nozzle at the first curve. As the hot dog raced down the hill, onions dropped from a mini-umbrella. At the next curve, relish was added, and finally, a slice of cheese was placed on top by small mechanical hands.

"Wow!" I exclaimed. "Everyone will love it!"

And love it, they did! Every one ate extra hotdogs just so they could try the machine again. Then afterwards, they took turns on Uncle Frank's special lawn chair!

Name _____

Complete the summary by adding phrases that help retell the story in a brief but complete manner.

• •

1. Today the speaker is excited because _____

    _____ .

2. The speaker is helping _____ .

3. Uncle Frank first asks the speaker to_____

    _____ .

4. The speaker is quite surprised when_____

    _____ .

5. Next, Aunt Beanie directs the speaker to_____

    _____ .

6. Then, Aunt Beanie demonstrates _____

    _____ .

7. After the demonstration, the speaker _____

    _____ .

Try this: Describe what you think Uncle Frank might invent for next year's barbeque. Draw and label a diagram of the invention.

41

Name _____

Read this advertisement. Complete the activity on page 43.

• •

You Need a Wuzzy Pet!

You do not need an animal to experience the joy of having a pet. Just get a Wuzzy Pet! It feels warm and fuzzy when you hold it. That is what makes it a "wuzzy." A Wuzzy Pet always comes when you call. Plus, you never have to feed or bathe it. Your Wuzzy Pet will even do tricks, like roll over or sit down. And it makes real animal noises. Choose your favorite. Get a Wuzzy Dog, a Wuzzy Cat, a Wuzzy Bird, or a Wuzzy Monkey. Or collect them all!

Wuzzy Pets are even better than the real thing. Now available at a toy store near you!

(Prices may vary. Some assembly required. Batteries are not included. Do not spill liquids on the toy or place it in water to avoid electric shock.)

You Need a Wuzzy Pet (cont.)

1. What is this advertisement trying to sell you?

   _____

   _____

2. What does the advertisement say is good about the product?

   _____

   _____

3. What does the advertisement say is bad about the product?

   _____

   _____

4. What does the advertisement warn about the product?

   _____

   _____

5. Write a short summary of this advertisement.

   _____

   _____

   _____

   _____

43

The Giant Sequoia

Read the passage Pay attention to the underlined words. You will use them to complete the activity on page 45.

• •

There are <u>forests</u> of <u>giant</u> trees in California. They are known as <u>sequoia</u> or redwood trees. A giant redwood can grow almost 76 meters (250 feet) tall. That is big as a skyscraper!

Giant redwoods can live for thousands of years. For the first 250 years, they look like small pine trees. When they are about 500 years old, they reach their full height. Sequoias are not only <u>tall</u>, they are also wide. Some are as big as 8 meters (25 feet) wide. You could not wrap your arms around that tree!

The first giant redwoods started growing about 200 <u>million</u> years ago. They were probably around when dinosaurs walked the earth. There used to be a lot more giant redwoods. They once grew all over North America. But, then the weather turned cold for awhile. These trees need warmth to grow. As a result, a lot of them died. Today, there are not many giant redwoods. They mainly grow in the <u>warm</u>, sunny state of California.

Forest fires are usually bad for trees. But, they sometimes help giant redwoods. The fire burns the small trees that grow in the shade of giant trees. That helps the small sequoia seedlings to grow better. This way, they get more sunlight and water. Before a fire, these growing redwoods had to share sun and water with other small trees.

Also, the heat of a forest <u>fire</u> opens up the cones that grow high up in the trees. The cones contain seeds. When the cones open, the seeds fall to the ground. They land in the soil and grow into new redwood trees.

When a giant sequoia dies, it falls onto the forest floor. Animals build homes in the fallen tree. As the tree breaks down, it helps other plants grow. Even though the tree has died, it is still an important part of the forest. Giant redwoods are some of the most amazing trees on Earth!

The Giant Sequoia (cont.)

Write a summary of the passage on page 44. Your summary should include all of the underlined words from the passage.

_____

_____

_____

_____

_____

_____

_____

_____

_____

_____

45

Answer Key

Page 4
1. boy; vegetables; 2. story; green; green; 3. grinned; 4. green food; 5. dessert; vegetables

Page 5
1. vet, dentist; 2. friend, alligator, cleaned; 3. dentist, insurance, prices; 4. vet, appointment; 5. vet, alligator, appointment

Page 6
1. A; 2. C; 3. A

Page 7
1. B; 2. C; 3. A; 4. A

Page 8
Maya, backpack, spelling, frog, report, monkey, pen, pencils, notebook, gum, sticky, new

Page 9
car, wheel, tires, rubber, wings, water, bridge, laughs

Page 10
Check: 1. C; 2. A; 3. B

Page 11
Cross out: the second, fourth, and eighth sentences; 1. B

Pages 12–13
Circle: the first verse, box the last verse; a. 1; b. 4; c. 5; d. 3; e. 2

Page 14
Answers may vary. Sample responses: 1. This article is about different kinds of seeds. 2. It grows into a palm tree. 3. A palm tree has a bigger seed than a redwood tree. 4. Willow seeds die quickly, while seeds from a lotus flower can last a very long time. 5. Answers will vary, but should include only the most important details.

Page 15
Circle: Summary B

Page 16
1. B; 2. C; 3. A

Page 17
Check: B, C, F, G

Pages 18–19
Circle: Summary D. Drawing should show a girl with her dog in an ice cream shop.

Pages 20–21
1. C; 2. The brothers tested their gliders and plane at Kitty Hawk. 3. Their first flight with a motor traveled 120 feet. 4. Answers will vary, but should include only the most important details.

Pages 22–23
Circle: Summary 1, Summary 3

Pages 24–25
old, sell, look, truck, grandparents, yo-yo, broken, teddy bear, friend, keep, old

Pages 26–27
a. 9; b. 10; c. 6; d. 5; e. 7; f. 2; g. 8; h. 1; i. 4; j. 3

Pages 28–29
1. A; 2. An illness left Helen Keller blind and deaf when she was a baby. 3. A teacher named Annie Sullivan helped Helen Keller learn how to speak. 4. Answers will vary, but should include only the most important details.

Pages 30–31
Cross out: We ate our favorite energy-boosting breakfast. We jumped very high and improved our drops. It was fun to pretend we were competing in a roller derby. I just love to "lead the pack" around the block. This is Makayla's favorite activity because she always seems to win. I lost interest quickly because I always seem to lose. Maybe a lucky rock would help me. Mom had made our favorite meal. I could eat macaroni and cheese almost any time. Makayla loves it, too.

Pages 32–33
a. 5; b. 2; c. 1; d. 4; e. 3. Drawing should show a car that matches the description in the article.

Pages 34–35
Circle: Cranebrook, Mareville, playing soccer, park, Katya, hot, Families, tie, the same

Pages 36–37
Answers may vary. Sample responses:
1. Cassie is a college girl asked to do a babysitting job. She is confident, determined, and a hard worker.
2. Bettie is a young and mischievous child who causes trouble for Cassie.
3. a. She put her hand in the chocolate pudding. b. She threw spaghetti into the air. c. She tracked spaghetti through the house.

Pages 38–39
1. Answers may vary. Sample responses: a. She dumped the bubble bath into the tub. b. She kicked blocks all over the room.
2. 4, 2, 1, 5, 3

Pages 40–41
Suggested Answers: 1. It is the day of the annual family barbeque at Frank and Beanie's. 2. Uncle Frank set up chairs. 3. put chairs around the pool and lawn. 4. a lawn chair he sat in flung him into the pool. 5. help in the kitchen. 6. Uncle Frank's new invention, a condiment-serving machine. 7. was very excited and told everyone about the invention.

Pages 42–43

Answers may vary. Sample responses:
1. This ad is trying to sell a toy called a Wuzzy Pet. 2. The ad says the toy feels warm and fuzzy, does tricks, and makes animal noises. 3. The ad says the toy requires some assembly and that prices may vary. Also, batteries are not included with the toy. 4. The ad says not to spill liquid on it or place it in water. 5. Answers will vary, but should include only the most important details.

Pages 44–45

Answers will vary, but should include only the most important details. Summaries should include the words forests, giant, sequoia, tall, million, warm, and fire.